Nicholas Benson

I Commissioned Some Wooden Luggage
and other poems

Afterword by Christopher Greger and James Penner

OPUNTIA

Opuntia is an imprint of Agincourt Press
Luigi Ballerini and Gianluca Rizzo, Editors
Agincourt Press is a non-profit organization chaired by Berardo Paradiso

All manuscripts are subject to peer review.

All rights reserved.

ISBN: 978-1-946328-44-1

AGINCOURT PRESS
P.O. Box 1039
Cooper Station
New York, NY 10003
www.agincourtbooks.com

© 2024 by Agincourt Press

Cover image: Silvio Zoratti, *Pileated Woodpecker*, 1962.
Photography by Heidi Kellner at www.zandkantiques.com

Contents

I Commissioned Some Wooden luggage   5

Afterword   63

Acknowledgments   71

In memory of my parents, Raymond and Shirley Benson

The word connects the visible trace with the invisible thing, the absent thing,
the thing that is desired or feared, like a frail emergency bridge flung over an abyss.

—Italo Calvino

Origin Story

out of sync. 5:55—dead or alive?
Plunge headfirst—wake up in
Hot Star Map. Touch anywhere to begin.

Even before already
considerable confetti
rude rigged & obscene

infernal machine.
Gains are fragile
fat is lean. What's stable

is mobile, porous
& clean. Arbitrary
constabulary, nonchalant

serene. Memento mori, sexy
& sly. Start out shy,
pee on the green.

Gastarbeiters & outpatients.
A thump, as under a bright lamp,
a body double, vision lost

in glare, left in random
pit stop. A bunch
of drunks, a moody novel

at the outset, you flare
& sprawl, issue an outburst
every so often. Lazy travel

writer accumulating days
& nights, you slip
away like vapor,

a trick card, come up and find
the tape erased, a faded number,
gone like a wave.

A blue noise,
a shimmer. It's not that they
want to kill you—it's that

they want to keep you alive. There
is just one returning beat.
Strap chin. Feet to street.

I commissioned some wooden luggage

With errata and exception, I love everything we did
& can recount the most minute detail,
the way you repeated partially

words I said, but forgave you,
not your native
language, to understand only later

what you were up to,
misplacing luggage,
sections of books, laundry,

hands of the clock.
No way to figure our growth
as it took on frigate proportions,

emissary of the court
arriving to filch deposition,
mumble an oath, time to lose

precious little as in haste I made off
in a diminished coat,
met a ship

with our name painted on.

Walked scab edifice scrubbed dirty
followed traces of indelible accent
through a facade full of holes like a wallet

Patched Trilby (too tight to fit) Scrum Sentinel and Sentimental Hat
along with Eyeglass Elegy
asking unending

Hoped for reply descending
in cross-hatch pattern,
secular portacross—

but got sprayed saliva instead
of cross porter. Become familiar with
the culture of baggage claim

become adept at the mumble rap,
retained crucifix design.
Here in Farcical City

the dailies elegantly orchestrate
a cornucopia of exquisite nostra culpas
while alongside an aisle the accumulator of imaginary slights

goes head to head
with the creator
of head-on-chest sonnets.

With paint mustache
virtual imbecile, suitcase unlatched

I disembark in the planet of desire
and wander off, involuntary stowaway

briefly quizzed at customs and shown the door.
Shuttle into town on moving corridor

music passing through soles and temples
pulsing in my chest like a glove—

an anesthetic life
migrating through my body, unwavering geese

missing an open engine; over burning land; at an artery
in your flank; by the obedient heart.

In present opiate, I was riding
Fluorescent *bici*
Through awful dust up
The grandeur of roadworks

It's *a biography of lies*
Said as though
Questionnaire's answers
Were sidewalk stain

I was shopping for
More black shoes
In spite of immersion coercion
And Intrepid Baroque

Building inhabitants look round
Recondite Fecund
& Records gone missing
At distraction police

The insecure saboteur
& Head Case
Put luggage down
At low tide

Red Herring
Said life intervenes
In numbing haste; and
Annalise Du Text

Installed behind
Protective irony
Pulled chain
On ricochet doggy

Wordless Exchange

You descend the marble staircase in front of your
mausoleum. Rapidly you emerge from
cloistered trees, potted plants dangling palpitating
fronds over balustrades. Leering gargoyles frame your entry into
the never-ending prison of the forward
march into subways and metropolitans, our shared
integument, the carapace that separates us. Although on other days,
the sudden collapse of structure scrambles the senses, so
that I roll coffee like a cigarette, don't notice
when I smoke it. Your fertility-goddess figure
plunges me into a communal apartment,
internecine strife, and the periphery, from this weirdly preserved
beaux-art tableau in the heart of the Quartier Latin. You say you've
already had husbands, kids, and a divorce— & *would you go out
and do the shopping now, please?*

Predicament

I don't sleep so much as submerge
into a network of substations traveling toward you

out on all lines to the final stop
out on the el in bright night air

past flower shops and beaches
parking lots and laundromats

the boardwalk by the sea
platform swept clean by moonlight—

without thinking, headed back in
the intricate weave

you stretch and spin me
I slide across like a bolt

you hold and contain—
electric cables extend

into the unknown heart—
into the exurbs, drowsy and alert,

focused and distracted. Above,
you burn with a cool flame.

*

Elemental,
you govern tides, light
my nights, ride coolly
across the sky. Sometimes

I think I see
all of you, a clean
beam, lucid
dream, mesmerizing

and unreachable. Other times,
you're more sly,
or shy, and part
of you is hidden. Deep

inside each pulse,
every dark stretch
lights up with the rhythm
of a glade in the sun

you remember
and reflect, even on
the coldest, most dreary
nights and days—

beyond a duvet,
behind a linen shroud,
an arras of damask,
a compost pile,

thick smoke
rises from the fields,
a faint sound,
a vanishing scent

on the periphery.
And this lilt, this sonar
lifting from trees
to the beyond,

penetrating deep
beneath. Alert
forager, ever-
optimistic

housebound traveler, these
lines are
for you.

*

A translation, an attempt
to catch, arrest, cross
language and space, a moment
that holds out, that resists

time's effects, and ours, to
recapture—that holds
out hope, against all attacks,
that makes an ally of time.

To move something, lovingly, carefully,
to carry it without spilling. So much
goes into the earth again,
and returns, training patience, wanting
to be named, recognized,

embraced—forgiven. For what?
For asking so much. Against the ignominy
of living, surrendering to
the deluge of days, to whatever
is prescriptive, prosaic.

Don't turn—return. Leaves
fall, clocks run back, words
submerge, trace
lines toward you. You are
in the sun. You remember: you reflect.

So many elsewheres make brilliant
your supple skin: stored

light, the shade
of a quiet lamp,

forgetful of its lumen.

What makes a place beautiful is
the moving through it —

the bulging arras of maples laughs,
the pale houses facing silence.

Shuttling by posts, lines, the boxes housing
the apparatus of our lives, we

enter something simple, strong,
and true—and just as soon, we've

known it all along;
it's used, and we're gone.

Sestina of remorse and fear

Signed that innocent-looking piece
of paper before I realized
it was my warrant, thought
it was my end. Furniture
on street, building
with shabby entry

to deteriorating entry,
ashtray garden, peace
disguised as mundane building,
late mail saying should've realized
when you found your furniture
rearranged; but you always think

you know better, until you think
it's too late, too late and entry
to the beyond is full of stacked furniture
rearranged Titanic-style; *pace
cuor mio*, it's not your fault I never realized
all the places we'd been, building

to this moment as a building
lifts its saurian head, *il pensiero*,
that drifts in ways only vaguely realized
but integral to those beyond the entry—
once inside, you can dream of peace,
you can sack out, supine on the furniture—

oh man, I could've been a tester of furniture,
I could've spent my time snoozing in some building
and getting paid, but instead I'm like a lost puzzle piece
that should use its heart instead of its head, that overthinking
fool who regularly screws up & isn't fit even to stand sentry
over whatever happened already. Sorry! —never realized

you really loved that girl, never realized
she wasn't like all the other bric-a-brac
thrown around like so many barriers in the entry
to block the public from the building,
left to stand in the contrapuntal undying thought
that redistributes each dissonant, smashed piece;

only realizing, when I saw our burning building
and my furniture in the street, only then thinking
entry may have been easy, but ever after, I'd have no peace.

Desire stands

under the tongue like a boy, while further
underneath, shades of green flow,
the silver-green, the yellow, blue,
and black—they wind up or down,
forth and back—more shades
of green than colors; as many
as our selves, pushers of paper
out of sight but not before they've
taken all the days; leaving the boy,
track signal flashing, dense
fog, distant whistle in green black.

What if you choose orange instead, twirl a twelve-petaled
daisy in mustard-tinged fingers until
its sheath spreads beneath? Can you take
colors back from the sky, distribute them at night? You turn
inside, the family surrounds you, and the cloak
upholds. On its carapace of lime, the town floats
over its breathing chasm, histories
rutting its sides, an honest
face. One day you wander down and find
the turnstiles locked, paths washed away, a rubble field
that spills toward bridges, burning orange exposure
where the hesitating path begins.

Blue void whirs triumphantly overhead
on dragonfly wings, the vanished thrumming
of the hummingbird, the violet net
cast between trees, can't escape –
one of the greens was blue, where pure element resides,
unutterable, ineradicable emptiness
of our migrating, sedentary selves: this shelf
of billowing blue in which I see you,
a tangle of subterranean and plain
view cables to festoon the chasm, keep
creatures and what they hold; as bluebird
night spreads her obscure tent of stone and spruce.

I look to the heart

of the moment and the curb
rises much too fast toward my eyes. To the far east
an index finger dislodges a coin from a daisy
faced handbag, places a nail on the slit
of a public phone. Lower
Broadway Wednesday
afternoon; calling
upper Broadway Tuesday evening—the eyes
of boys described by Cavafy
murmur from the face of a woman
suddenly swinging by me: seduction a killing
gaze, a fractional upset in the lull
of shopping, the sleep
of sex awakening, bursting the truce
of wallets, caressed
and slapped shut, a brief
aperture in the rotation, the moment
passing as though lives
never touched. In shunned
bodies, the mourners glide
through aisles turnstiles alleys,
between counters, amidst
the screaming prophecies of theaters,
promises fading to a few
rudimentary facts, scratched
celluloid, brain
mere parchment, glance

of girls made
language again: lifelong
register of loss and gain.

Spores

A woman who looks just like Boccioni's mother
is staring at her in a drawing done by her son. She wears

that Italian quilted coat they all wear, and carries
that stylish handbag they all have, and has

the same curled hair strong cheekbones grim chin hawk nose
below incisive eyebrows—

unabashed she hesitates
between admiring and appalled: I can't tell. She looks up

close in at the drawing
straight on then at an angle

and can't seem to get past it
or to know how she feels

about seeing herself in another life so long ago—
the drawing is called *La madre*—

and maybe that is her mother, or her *grand*mother: it was done in 1909—
maybe that is her *great*-grandmother; the idea I might ask occurs

as she strolls past, walks on, ink on
paper, marks left

of strides but
as though never here, her breath ascending

evaporating like lines of slacks, her legs elegant and soundless,
without discernible expression through the spiraling hall

Discrete entanglement

Plot?
Yes, OK: as in a landscape by Klee, as in

his 'aide-mémoires'—
Southern Gardens—

brief blurts
of color and light.

Familiar,
uncertain frames

of shapes, buildings, dreams
burst and reconstructed on an incandescent, lucid plane.

It resembles the surface of a reservoir. And its surroundings: a deliberate slope, and up its sides: a mess.

But richer, with threads,
the bits retained,

crunched light, the shreds
still attached somehow

to something that coheres—
lost worlds.

OK, yes: to contain them. Build a frame;
they escape.

Chanson forensic

Caught smoking
mom's cigarettes,
held by the hand.

Why's it called
French kissing?
Thought I'd find

out. She allowed me to see
why we feel around
in the darkness of the park, in

the blinding sun, and when
I find you there, only then
does oblivion desist, curiously

hang back, like an extra
behind the scenery. You said
don't frown, don't

look down, this
leads to light. You
were digressive,

a pavilion, fresh
gravel, they're never
finished working—but I confuse

what I knew with
the distant evocation.
We didn't know each other, not

at the same time, although
years later, I see you walking on
the streets of the city, uptown,

west side, your
producer at your side, later in
the year of your death—as in a dream,

watch you touch
barely down in
our exhausted metropolis, brilliantly lit.

□

One dives down
a canal without a point of interest,

another insists on this place and none other,
but it's absurd—

this rankling debate, as though opposites—
What about that canal?

In the Lido—nothing there to meet the eye—
corrugated plastic and metal facade

on rococo plaster, bath house
shenanigans, your hot hands—

one dives deeper
and recedes, becomes an address.

Your tactic was
to make of love

a mathematics, to parcel out time
withheld from us, as though that way

we could have it without responsibility.
Turns out you're right, we live in

the distribution of what tied us together.
These sheer drops lead to light.

☐

This sun: the days you have.
The grass: the years that pass.

There has to be a body: evidence
of work. Your smile

flashes again: a beacon instead
of an answer.

There is a bad connection somewhere.

Fraternizing wastelands;
communicating storms.

□

After all
there must be something
in the place of
no-thing

this doesn't mean you
mean nothing.
This doesn't mean nothing,
even if this 'don't mean a thing'—

*You mean thin*g*!* catcall on
a humid night, moon-face turned
toward the other side
of the earth—

after all, there must
be something

☐

11:00. Orpheus
flips through the channels—

static; tornado; the perfect mattress;
antacid.

       Orpheus, again—
in the garage

seeking solitary refuge in a parked car.
I wanna thank you, John

—sudden twang of hokum brings tears to the eyes. Dumpster
diver—your responsibilities await you.

       Orph-
no signal.

Notion escapes. All you can see
of his house

is the garage door. *Orpheus,*
fickle Orpheus.

>*Eurydice*: stay in the garage. I know night

has taken my sleep, that Venus
appears larger in the night sky
before she is in fact closer to us.

There is logic in this, even if no one
knows the reason
sleep from me

has taken. *What shall last then if*
all this and you
are gone? The endings, the

last shall last;
and that's all?

☐

In her metaphors already the retro-
spective foretaste of her death. She looks
back from the dead, from the
photo, and

her songs hang in
midair. Eurydice with Orpheus's gift, I see her
walking, producer
at her side, simple

angel, upper
west—appropriated
by illusions you
created? Impossible

to say whether illusion was your appearance here
or your (more pervasive) non
being now. If your gaze
still hangs before me, between tenement

and street, vapor from
underground, already singing to us
after you had left, before
your death: you have become the shape of our story.

Ode to Lost Time

Let's study the cap: says contents
in seventeen languages

Orpheus & Eurydice played on the stage
in Camus's *Plague*

over & over until the lead expired
Goldenrod indefatigably march up the hill

and suddenly they're here between the defeated iris and quince
speaking of the body her enunciation

snaps shut I think
like my dad's black briefcase

in 1976. Like the way her r's
slur as she sloshes

over some phrase. Onerous & grave,
I have a vague

recollection of opening it, and—nothing
into which decades slip—into which

somebody might take
her by the hand, guide her through

this purling merchandise, to lose her
amidst the sweltering populace, the lubricious

largesse of these severed heads—anything to detain
the burgeoning tocsin, the fly-buzzing

song of dread—Lord, lead us to
the lovely ladies lurking by the fresh-cut nosegays, fondling

tufts of daisies placed repetitively, perfectly in
the slender-tipped vases

of street shrines—
while your visage slips through the portal—

(prohibited content)

                          Goldenrod march
up and down the hill

hazardous bursts
of pollen spend

themselves—is there any other
than this cursed way

of giving? Still I camp
in your curbsides, the truck

and trailer stops
of sand and salt (mostly sand),

the salacious striptease
of strict analogies—

say *hibiscus*
the next word is *frangipani*;

say *bougainvillea*
the next word is shut up—

constant bluff, leaf shower—but may
be there's

a way to
scratch through

to another:
plan it all along

but never lived there...

                        Here too,
escort and chase, your visage

slips through the center lane: saffron red
street light reflecting

off wet flanks of shepherds
that merge

into surrounding bushes and bichons
& now you're another

island of light whose number
connects a complete stranger,

& says: reduce
yourself to essence—

witness
& vanish—

and I: thank you
(dobermans strain the leash)

Direct, diffuse

I wanted you and you said
have you got a coffee

Hell yes, but I'm embarrassed
I drink the stuff all the time and it keeps returning

you should be happy—
an aside: the silly crown

we wear
—I don't think you copy—

reads no vice, no way, innocent & honest
it's starting to get colder—

delicate economy
of want & need again.

Second round.
As in Buñuel, explosions

replace speech, lithe
terrorist, no need to knock

or ring, what makes you think
you're discrete? I see you through

my periscope, you fill
the hallway. How are there

three of you?
And each scene

is a night scene, Shanghai
occupied by the Japanese—

maybe because you
taunt me with your knees winking

across the table. The problem
is detachment

lies everywhere in intimate disguise,
desire infiltrates

the bored walkway
between tortured trees, sticks

chimney pipe through the boudoir
and filches compact, pockets

false eyelash (anything
to get found out)

Round trips

She painted her toenails red. Her butler
waxed his mustache. He wasn't
her butler. He was in the service
of the crown prince of Bhopal. Italian,
she had married at fourteen
in order to give me sleepless nights.

"I want you to never forget me" she whispered,
hot hand resting lightly on my arm.

A draft emanated from the interior loggia of heroes
and miniature shade palms
in the muted skylit aviary.

"You may call again."

Summer. In the park of dusty chestnuts, she bared
her cool arms. "But don't you ever have work to do?"

The ripples in the fountain
ceased. A crow flapped off,
a startled attaché case. In the courtyard,
her father sat on a three-legged stool,
grinding his knives.

Everyone transiting on

the same escalator,
with one arm lifted
to the sides of their faces,
closed, in vague comradeship
purely based
on language, what tears
them apart. I suspect
everybody of the murder
of the self. You and I are in
the whirling orb of continuous
derailment, the play
ground. The vertigo of fathers they
mostly keep to themselves. There's
a strange man,
has a navy suit coat
w/blue shirt white collar
jewelry goatee ski hat
and sideburns, sweating constantly
behind a train robber's mustache.
It doesn't add up,
but there it is. For him, what was once
effortless, simply said and seen,
had on arrival become
something arduous, to work
on all over again. Hermes exhausted
by the demands of the contract
at last damns the wondrous armature

of this city infested
with fruitless subterfuges,
stealing from under their faces, hiding
in plain sight, unleashing
a grin words never fill. Instead they
make monuments, dam it up, find themselves
on the other side. Put an
official seal over the place where—
crosses, no—crosses never
cross out anything; every
thing they slice through more
alive than ever. The wry
look, the grin, rip
in the glinting armor
through which we discern
what lay dormant before, burst open,
found legs and dashed off—in the fabric
an irruption, scattering pigeons,
children, and nannies in the park;
while you, undisturbed in
a sailor's hat with white tassel
and crescent moon smile,
wander off
beside me, star-strewn.

A man reaches out

forever to his child
to his most clever self

Says to his progeny Go now Don't stay
It was all a dream

My past does not exist
and you Are

As long as man puts forth seed in the breach
And wine flows through the gate
And the primal flowerbed buds
Glows in tresses dark bright limitless
So shall the heart of man bay and sunder
A traveler in the heart as at first

Bread will heal the wound
Tears will salt it again
Rain will pour on his head
Sun will beat it like stone

All will be one which will be gone as though lost
He will hurt just the same with identical pain

Leave, poor fathers, a plan of your pathways
since as its sense bruises our flesh and brain
it may tell of the typical wound inside.

My Colosseo

A wind blew from you
into the seven hills, it crossed
the drifting, sleeping towns, sent
remains to scud through
your centuries, so that even
these beefy gladiators can't see
what time it is (except one I saw pull
a cellphone out of his pants).

Your eroding face
birthed whole neighborhoods
where pollard-lined avenues
drunkenly wind from and down
to you, spilling buses, mopeds,
trams and the rain
that never quite keeps
the exhaust in check.

Everyone goes straight
to you, the place in the middle
where they dream of periphery,
while you patiently float
above their peripatetic dreams,
partly on bedrock, partly
on silt. There's nothing so
unusual about that,

but to have always seen
your face, hovering
on its couch of sand and stone,
since anyone can remember...
Like everyone, once I loved
your innermost, open
parts, exposed not so much to
the elements as to cats and paint,

a corrugated plastic and tin
people's beloved latrine. Rank
with copulation, darkness and light
held apart where earth and its abuse
intertwined. Still today it's in
your maw, down in the viscera, amidst
your groin, in all the exquisite creases
of your everlasting crown,

that people find your—their—
vitality, headphones on. I prefer
the spaces between pillars, the
ever-changing atmosphere that
infiltrates these spans of stone,
and it's never been
any different; anyone
could always get a ticket. Death,

love, in strict dark and on display; mostly death, & with
a guarantee, often, or the promise

of a riot at least, drearily simulated now
by the tourist horde that gushes under your broad rim
sprouting bristles and spears, unruly and green,
nary a silver lance or trim sword. I gaze toward
all I loved, secure within your shabby
allure, your archaic embrace. O my suburb.

...

Everyone knew, but forgot,
how those men were either dumb
but physically imposing, or
prevented from advancing because
of some political mischance—
prisoners of war, slaves, or
out of luck and (nearly) lives, they
thought they may as well make the last attempt
last. It sounds almost glamorous now: the chosen,
paraded forth to the wild acclamation of the people...
ignorant and refined alike emerging in
sifting clouds of dung-light, along the runnels of the stalls,
filing into the sand and sawdust-filled
arena, a clatter of scabbards, iron and leather,
hollering incense and the stench
of animal and human, the rhythm
of swerving blades splitting sinew,
blood that might have sprayed the first row. If

the vanquished wasn't dead, the crowd
might give life back until the next
engagement; beyond mercy, the victor
would remain. I looked on the slate today
and saw my name.

Landscape

> *after Ker-Xavier Roussel,* Paysages *(1897)*
> *and Paul Gaugin,* Red Cow *(1889)*

This light
darkens. Etruscan
almost, the frieze-like
poplars and wheat, the sickle
and scythe, one sharpening the blade,
one as ever bowed
to reap, the lurid
red cow in the foreground
reassuring somehow, nature's calm
bounty, the contented cat
crouching beneath, a woman
with a pitcher bending
toward the viewer, leaning almost
outside the picture frame.

Mooring

after Joan Mitchell (1971)

In indistinct land, on water, a line extends
one holds onto amidst color, washes and striations,
iridescent neon bouncing in cool clamor, smoke
of fires that ride like hats in
evening ash: the bright mystery cascades
inert on the retina, threatening oblivion from
its silent perch, a quiet dimension from which no
thing is heard; except, mute and humble, still
a place that one can ride, like light.

[the label, the *etichetta* has something like a dhow on it, charcoal script on an eggshell canvas field, inscrutable verbiage, symbols like an anchor, a pair of eyes, marine heliotrope instead of information]

I always said that if you look at something closely enough, and for long enough, you will see in it what you wish. Lately, though, it seems this works the other way around. I was looking at a mundane *etichetta* but no doubt one that had not changed for some time. I was interrupted while scraping away the residue left over from making the previous day's pigments. The color arrived in the eyes of one of the hired girls. Hired to model her arms, what surprised me about her, so that I ignored her bare arms and focused there intensely instead for the whole afternoon, was the outward sign of a bashful soul, the concealed truth that can not hide. In the shifting light of the studio – a piercing yellow ray, a golden fan, the saturated giallorino of the midday rest, then the saffron backdrop of the day's long end – I beheld twin pools of sapphire, cobalt, phosphorescence, mica, moonlight, lava, cornflowers, a steep slope of comfrey, a copse of borage, bluebirds that vanish in the dusk, lashes softly closing in their wake like weary pine boughs. I knew she had been brought there to provoke me, but I could not turn away my eyes, brick-red, oxidized, badly cellared for a long time. My tired skeleton, svelte as a salamander, was an eel escaped from the lagoon into the bewildering ocean. Confronted by my fate, unaware, the oracle spent, the temple unoccupied for such a long time, minerals in heaps, crumbling from the pulsing (*if you look at something*) walls, my mind turned away from everything I knew and found true lapis lazuli, ultramarine, brought in by the dhows and delivered to my studio as twin wells of lazuline from which I shall never be parted.

[old burlap with an indistinct black corolla: the faded image of a grille interlaced with dried flowers, vine leaves, and small dun-colored birds with red and green streaks or smudges, crowns or joker's peaked hats; the controlled scribble of handwriting in an obscure language]

The brotherhood of the knife, they call it. *I prefer the sisterhood of the spoon*, I don't say, across the table where S– flings a brace of pigeon, corncrake, wagtail, chiffchaff, the smell of the meadow still upon them, hearts still racing. I must not show them I'm angry. *This is a common skylark!* I said last time, hoping to dissuade them. *Not once you're finished with it*, A– responded, while S– picked his teeth with the point of his knife and stared at me as though he'd just realized that I was capable of speaking. Anyway, it's true: every year there are fewer, just as there are fewer fields – so common, so rare. Through their subterfuge are these contraries confused. Perhaps this is the better way; the way everybody likes it; this works in our favor; our survival is in this. Goodbye sister, willow warbler, goodbye lover, domestic thrush. The names all that remains. Today I wandered from my den to find "Feast of the Thrush" posted everywhere, drunken revelry spilling over balustrades and around the Corso in the evening, everybody dancing in period costume, clouds of smoke and sparks from the overstuffed busts and braziers where the birds, trussed and docile, elegantly rest, brilliantly arrayed like nobles at a theatre set alight with bloodless precision. In miniature script that only expert eyes can decipher, in place of *aythya nyroca*, *anthus pratensis*, *turdus philomelus*, I write the names of those who drink this down.

Night book

The upside-down book
turns inside out. All the old days
rush by raining great gray columns,
big gloomy buildings where dusty winds
originate. Buses splash through dark
deep puddles, sparks crackle along
trolley cables. Clenched teeth
of the neighborhood stray,
not rabid, just afraid.

Her glare undressed, looked off,
returned, zipped up, went home.
Monuments dream along the wall.
A garden hose uncoils, notes bend
from the window, fall through leaves.
Plenty of dogs are barking
in their sleep. I was there
only briefly. I spent
the night walking.

The moon
is a scythe sledding
from left to right,
and the railings, deeply respectful,
gloam and boast of its flight.
Nubes of no weight like polite applause
skate past. Neon signs blink, tugboats honk,

oceanliners light strings of color
as four or five airliners intersect.

Everywhere you look
there are cardboard boxes,
buildings cut out quickly —
masses of people in each window,
masses of windows blink back blindly —
wherever we look there are reading lights,
jetliners wingtips,
hardhats beacons,
and in portholes the moon.

Someone must be there
holding up both hands to support the sun.
The world is a star floating
millions of centuries from its double
source and companion
like a file turned inside out, strands
swaying through the eye of the public,
measured out in prescribed doses,
in private lives.

It is a scream for successful brokers,
while the broken refuse to rediscover
the eternal verities, to please
him, her, god, mom, dad, teacher —
would rather whip around a corner
with mad glee if you see someone

floating, a world torn off like a wrong
number, a page written in haste, in invisible
ink, an undecipherable alphabet — *deja vu*

cut off with a slam. Holy matrimony
between cloud and ocean. The mountain
has gone into remission. Gorgeous in moonlight
the path leads to a clearing, starlight daytime telephone —
rings around a traffic circle, suffocation birds
awaken, creeping upstairs small guest,
squirrel with a candle,
remarkable understandable. Earth declares
itself independent.

Marvelous curve of the body (hers)
turned aside deliberately inviting
comparison with a cool current
changing direction, surf gently rippling
in the narrows of design,
switching toward the delicate meadow
where life is organized into rows,
the spokes of a wheel
radiating from an original form.

Even here
where fields continue,
one forgets end or beginning
direction, day, whose property and why —
there is a temporal uncategorizeable something

pure vast and spatial
like a blank pause
no one can say for how long because
the clocks have stopped —

and the countryside resumes, its evident order
consisting of course of properties
holdings landmarks
with meanings transferred
through people over time handed down
we perceive this sort of thing
maybe if we're from there we even recall some secrets
behind each face of normalcy
looking back, or mirror

mentioning the hallucinogenic green,
fields and lawns, late May
after days of rain: the sun
lacerates the grateful lances
of grass in polite curtsey
below the elegant drapes of alacrity
trees that nobly grace porches
of freshly washed air
spanked brightly

as though by an absurdly self-contained actor
bent upon seeing the world whole
every day. Haven't we become
too accustomed, trading in

talents, as though feelings — as though
no means of recompense existed? And all
we desire to show ourselves
capable and true: each of us
an original astral body.

Don't say

every contact
cuts one way
or another, and always
what pulls us together

keeps us apart.
Accident or design? When I see
you in a corner, our belated shroud
splits all the way down. We think

there's no shame in what's
not said, not done. And so
the days, the blanks between
these numbered piers extend,

irresistible ordinary
enchantments; the nights click past,
an analog track, your
way back. Found on the binary.

I wanted

I wanted to visit the graveyard—
*The Third Cemetery
of the Spanish and Portuguese Synagogue Shearith Israel
in the City of New York 1829-1851*—

but was distracted by the billboards and construction raging
the constant crunch of demolition
somewhere a jackhammer the flash of a welder
dark limousines pulling in and out of the adjacent parking lot

a vast dark blot where the owners are never seen—
behind a fence only a dog could love
all the stones had fallen in
and were strewn over the luckless grass—

my eyes were drawn to the spectacle
of a working lunch aboard a stationary vehicle
in the fragmented miracle of sidewalk
split into millions of disposable parts

as clerks customers clients and patrons
channeled and conducted
docile and distracted
over a temporary plywood bridge

continued unabated conversations with the absent

The Investigation

—they regularly update every thing, so that whole ways of saying
are eradicated; but not entirely. What happens is this: our memories
are wiped, and in their place: *what*

again. Words bring meditation on. Thinking
makes pleasure, which part of us says is *all wrong*. I've done
nothing to earn you, just struggled beside you,

yet we're apart. An original and a
translation. What I wanted to say goes the other way. Paths cross. One goes uphill,
one down. It looked like eight p.m. at three, and wrote in a green

notebook *A big front's frayed edge is
blowing down here*. The same blue field brackets
unusual things, brought into the open—stray guitar, the humming

of a tuneless neighbor—someone left, & came
back because, maybe, they forgot their coat; or wanted to
retrieve something. I have this terrible feeling each

word is an island that will disappear. An austere
efflorescence into another life. Events split. One escapes,
one leaves. Stage right and left. There are two of us

at least, and never the same. Once I had you, yet still
wanted you even more. You loved me later
but couldn't say. So it all ends. And begins—

The catbirds

are convinced that I
love only them, or at least that I'm
on their side, because I've
planted so much they like,
but three just got trapped
inside the netting, and forgot
to eat the rest of the berries,
thinking only of escape. Their wings
still intact, I released them, and now
they run through a complex string of calls,
surprised, happy, pissed. They say
they're ready to do it all over again. They've got
the whole valley to play in, but it's this
disheveled garden, these berries they won't abandon.

The finches

Orioles and warblers gone, overgrown
fields fill with finches, the mullein
long faded and long, black-eyed susans
saying summer's at its peak,
means it's almost over, through
the leathery stalks they swarm and stumble,
intoxicated and alert, they dip and dart
after each other in pairs and en masse,
the finches, filling the spaces between the yellow
and green with their minute flickering
black yellow and white, the filchers of seed momentarily
here, never really still, the last light dims
and they appear to have vanished – gray
does not interest them and it's gray now
with black advancing from within the trees,
not the cheerful ones astray in the field the finches swarm
and mingle in, but dense brooding forest clumps
of evergreens; soon the finches will move
into another scene, subtly shifting flowers and grasses
evidence next spring of their passing.

The Moment

Does it ever come?

*

ah!....there it goes....

*

Look at that pink! Luminescent tufts glide imperceptibly across above

deepening green-black spires of pine, and upright, splaying fans of leaves striate

darkening blue like the vertex of an egg: a fragility that can only mean

night plunged into stupor already

Envoi

Pen, it is darkly amusing
how I fear to lose you. So little can make
everything seem to vanish,
that it can. Yet only

you hold firm, reassuring,
indulgent soul, willing
to cancel mistakes, happy
to make them. You return

the hand's embrace, stoic ally
in the storm of airy non
chalance and dread that is
the page, all day; and I

would plunge, merge
with your solemn night
road song, making it up
along with you.

Afterword

While backpacking in Europe as a teenager in the 1980s, Nick Benson stumbled on a window display in a Venetian gallery that caught his eye: it featured a beautifully carved duffle-bag sculpted from wood, complete with drawers. For the itinerant Benson, this *objet d'art* was a source of fascination: "you could keep your travel bag by your bed and be ready to go, but it could also be a useful piece of furniture…I would have commissioned some wooden luggage, if not for the price tag… instead it became a metaphor and took on a life of its own. I didn't realize it then, but it's the embodiment of wanting opposing things at once. It seems to sum up this permanent sense of duality—rootedness and restlessness" (Interview with Benson, January 19, 2024).

The longing for the state of fluid detachment that travel often affords is a recurring motif in *I Commissioned Some Wooden Luggage*. For Benson, life in an "in-between state" began early, during a childhood in a series of locales—Ankara, Moscow before the fall of the Soviet Union, and Belgrade when it was still part of Yugoslavia: "growing up as a diplomat's kid means I certainly didn't live like a Turkish kid or a Russian kid, for example. It made me very curious, and aware of the privileges that I had... but linguistically and culturally I lived apart, in the international community. This left me with a desire to know places where I didn't belong, and the language of those places, because I never really belonged where we were living." The state of being perpetually on the outside and not having firm roots in one place inspired Benson to write poetry: "in retrospect, for me poetry was like a third language, symbolic and indirect—yet also more concise. Joseph Brodsky called poetry 'a terrific mental acceleration.'[1] It's both more concise and more allusive, or digressive—the fact that it doesn't have to serve a utilitarian aim means you can say things in poetry that don't belong anywhere else." Benson's notion of poetry as a "third language" is reflected in many of his poems. It's not an accident that many of the writers who have influenced him are poets whose works he read in translation—Eugenio Montale, Czeslaw Milsosz, Zbigniew Herbert, and Wislawa Szymborska, among others.

Benson, who translates from the Italian, cites the act of translation as analogous to the act of writing poetry. In his poem "Predicament," the reader encounters a startling definition of translation: "an attempt/to catch, arrest, cross/language and space, a moment/that holds out, that resists//time's effects, and ours, to/re-

---

[1] *Joseph Brodsky: Conversations*, edited by Cynthia L. Haven (University Press of Mississippi, 2002) pp. 121-130; p. 121.

capture—that holds/out hope, against all attacks,/that makes an ally of time." Reflecting on this passage, Benson notes, "in retrospect, I'm attempting to grapple with this duality, where you are both in the moment and out of it, and time almost seems to fold over. You are in the present and the past at the same time—but you can only express that in a poem."

In addition to the theme of translation, Benson likens the act of poetic composition to a form of mental photography: "there are a lot visual stimuli in the poems, almost psychological moments that are fixed or rest on a visual frame. An analogy might be to a cinematic frame, part of a narrative, with a particular arrangement, and that's what I'm recording. There are elements of biography, but they're inseparable from imagination."

The cinematic perspective can be found in a central poem of the collection, "My Colosseo." The poet apostrophizes the venerable ancient monument: "Your eroding face/birthed whole neighborhoods/where pollard-lined avenues/drunkenly wind from and down/to you, spilling buses, mopeds,/trams and the rain/that never quite keeps/the exhaust in check." The speaker's one-sided conversation becomes an affectionate flirtation in the fourth stanza: "but to have always seen/ your face, hovering/on its couch of sand and stone,/ since anyone can remember…/Like everyone, once

I loved/your innermost, open/parts, exposed not so much to/the elements as to cats and paint [...]." The poet's address to the ancient monument morphs into an eerie meditation on history and the passage of time. With cinematic precision, the speaker recreates an ancient scene in the *Colosseo*: "along the runnels of the stalls,/filing into the sand and sawdust-filled/arena, a clatter of scabbards, iron and leather,/hollering incense and the stench/of animal and human, the rhythm/of swerving blades splitting sinew,/blood that might have sprayed the first row." Benson's surreal language juxtaposes image, sound and olfactive references to anchor us in the present and past at the same time. The poem ends with the speaker encountering an image of his own mortality: "I looked on the slate today and saw my name." In discussing the juxtaposition of contemporary and archaic elements in his poems, Benson commented: "I grew up in gritty capital cities that had the feeling of being both contemporary and ancient, and dilapidated—but none of them were Rome, unfortunately! Rome is a fantastic mixture of the sublime and the shabby…because it's so ancient and lived in at the same time, Rome shows how a place is concentrated time. It's totally distracting, but it makes you see layers." In response, Benson's poetry contains layers—historical, cultural and linguistic—and allows the reader to experience the sense of the present vexed by an uncomfortable relationship with the past.

Benson's fascination with historical locales and their subliminal persistence in contemporary urban life is also reflected in the poem "I Wanted." In this poem, the speaker sets out to visit the "Third Cemetery of the Spanish and Portuguese Synagogue Shearith Israel in the City of New York 1829-1851." However, rather than leading to contemplation, his excursion is disrupted "by the billboards and construction raging/ the constant crunch of demolition/somewhere a jackhammer the flash of a welder/dark limousines pulling in and out of the adjacent parking lot." The speaker is overwhelmed by the urban mayhem that churns on all around the cemetery, a dilapidated, slender remnant of another time. The poet looks on as a parade of "clerks customers clients and patrons/channeled and conducted/docile and distracted/over a temporary plywood bridge//continued unabated conversations with the absent." The poem is a meditation on not only the passage of time, but the anomie of the present and how people fail to connect with others who inhabit the same space. Benson commented on this theme in his urban poems: "the city is a congestion of these discrete consciousnesses that are not connecting, but are sharing the same space, and there is palpable tension there—it can be galvanizing, and it can also be frustrating or threatening depending upon the situation...no one there took any notice of the cemetery. What struck me then is the irony of how people are less connected with what's right around them, and less connected with each other in a real way, the more they're connected through technology. A typical example is when you find people sharing the same space, but they're all online, or they're talking loudly even, but not to someone who's actually there. I was in New York recently with my daughter, and we sat down at a communal table in a busy but somehow still quiet cafe on 9th Avenue—and there was a woman sitting right across from us and talking right at us—but into thin air... That's an unremarkable scene these days, but it struck me how different it was some 30 years ago, when I was going to college in New York, as my daughter is now."

Throughout this collection, poems span a sometimes vertiginous gap between past and present. Many of them are rooted in a single fraught moment in which "the present is so full of the past that it's somehow both," as Benson remarks. "You're in the moment of writing, but the poem is also full with whatever has happened before, and it's your reading now that bridges these gaps. I should say your reading is an *attempt* to bridge these gaps, because nothing is assured... as Calvino wrote, language is 'a frail emergency bridge thrown over an abyss'."[2] Benson's poetry often spans this in-between space, as he crosses from one locale to another while seldom remaining in one fixed position.

---

[2] Italo Calvino, *Six Memos for the Next Millennium*, 'Exactitude,' trans. Patrick Creagh (Vintage, 1993) p. 77.

For this poet, witnessing a work of art is itself a generative act, one from which a number of poems in this volume emerge. In the poem "Landscape," standing before Gauguin's *Red Cow*, Benson confronts another series of gaps – not only between the work of art and the viewer, but between the depicted image and its object. Indeed, Benson's own poems spring from the tension he identifies in the works of art he is attracted to: "I find a painting especially intriguing when the line between representational and abstract is blurred. What you're seeing is the artist grapple with the precariousness of the real, and an analogous process of representation and internalization happens in a poem. So with Joan Mitchell and the painting *Mooring*, the artwork seems to fold over time and consciousness and that creates a space that allows the viewer in." In the poems about paintings, the speaker is keenly interested in filling in the gaps, allowing both reader and viewer to become active participants in the production of meaning.

Benson's experience as a translator of Italian poetry underlies this collection, though perhaps nowhere is it explored with such myriad resonances as in "The Investigation." In it Benson writes "I have this terrible feeling each//word is an island that will disappear. An austere/efflorescence into another life." Of this poem, Benson remarked that it is partially a record of "grappling with the transient nature of experience, and the ephemeral connection between people, which is never reconcilable. There is the *now*, but you could say even the now is dictated by what's outside the moment."

Ultimately, the arc of poems in *I Commissioned Some Wooden Luggage* traces this perennial vexation of our mortal lives, finding resolution in the act of writing itself. As the volume progresses, the locus of poetic attention spirals outward from an interior landscape to points outside, whether on a gallery wall or in the environment. The collection concludes with a brief series of poems engaging the natural world – catbirds, finches, the moment of the sun's departure from the horizon. Through urban dislocation, through the dislocations of travel, there is a final return to rootedness and the nature that surrounds us, even while, as in the poem "The finches," the sun sets and the finches, *never really still, move into another scene.*

Christopher Greger and James Penner
January 19, 2024

Acknowledgments

Two poems in this volume—"Mooring" and "Envoi"—were presented by Maria Grazia Calandrone on the RAI Radio Tre program *Poesia statunitense contemporanea* (March 2023). I am grateful to Maria Grazia for her insightful comments, and for her wonderful translations of these poems into Italian.

I owe much to those who read the poems in this volume at various stages, and always offered invaluable advice: my brother Michael; Rick Jackson; Natasha Sajé; and David Wojahn.

For their belief in this book, I am grateful to Luigi Ballerini and Gianluca Rizzo, the editors of Agincourt Press, as well as their colleagues Beppe Cavatorta and Federica Santini.

Huge thanks to Christopher Greger and James Penner for elevating this collection with their collaboration.

Above all, this book would not have been possible without the constant love and support of my family: my wife Lili, and our children, Katharine and Hezekiah.

The title poem is dedicated to Mebane Robertson (1967-2020).

Chanson forensic is dedicated to Kirsty MacColl (1959-2000).

About the author

Nicholas Benson was born in West Germany in 1966 and grew up in Yugoslavia, Turkey, and the USSR. He holds an MA in Italian (Middlebury, 1991), a PhD in Italian (New York University, 1999), and an MFA in Writing (Vermont College of Fine Arts, 2009). He has published translations, poems, and essays in many journals. His translations include Attilio Bertolucci's *Winter Journey* (Parlor Press, 2005); Aldo Palazzeschi's *The Arsonist* (Otis Books/Seismicity Editions, 2013), for which he was awarded an NEA Translation Fellowship; in collaboration with Elena Coda, Scipio Slataper's *My Karst and My City and Other Essays* (Lorenzo Da Ponte Library/University of Toronto Press, 2020), which was awarded the John Florio Prize by the Society of Translators (UK); and Maria Grazia Calandrone, *(°) – seed and other poems*, edited by Beppe Cavatorta (forthcoming from Opuntia).

About the critics

Christopher Greger is the author of *Aestheticism and the Femme Fatale* and *Yeats and the Sacred Book*, as well as the novel *The Other Worlds*. He is Professor of English and Humanities at City College San Francisco.

James Penner is a contributor to the *Los Angeles Review of Books*. He is the author of *Pinks, Pansies, and Punks: the Rhetoric of Masculinity in American Literary Culture* and the editor of *Timothy Leary: the Harvard Years*. He is an Associate Professor of English at East Los Angeles College.

AN OPUNTIA BOOK

Published by Agincourt Press ©2024,
New York, NY, in an edition of
200 copies. Design by
Gary Green. Typeset
in Garamond
Pro.

www.ingramcontent.com/pod-product-compliance
Lightning Source LLC
Chambersburg PA
CBHW030534080526
44586CB00011B/441